Would You Rather Gross! Edition

Scott Matthews

© Copyright 2019 - All rights reserved.

The content contained within this book may not be reproduced, duplicated or transmitted without direct written permission from the author or the publisher. Under no circumstances will any blame or legal responsibility be held against the publisher, or author, for any damages, reparation, or monetary loss due to the information contained within this book. Either directly or indirectly. You are responsible for your own choices, actions, and results.

Legal Notice:
This book is copyright protected. This book is only for personal use. You cannot amend, distribute, sell, use, quote or paraphrase any part, or the content within this book,
without the consent of the author or publisher.

Disclaimer Notice:
Please note the information contained within this document is for educational and entertainment purposes only. All effort has been executed to present accurate, up to date, and reliable, complete information. No warranties of any kind are declared or implied. Readers acknowledge that the author is not engaging in the rendering of legal, financial, medical or professional advice.

The content within this book has been derived
from various sources. Please consult a licensed professional before attempting any techniques outlined in this book.

By reading this document, the reader agrees that under no circumstances is the author responsible for any losses, direct or indirect, which are incurred as a result of the use of the information contained within this document, including, but not limited to, — errors, omissions, or inaccuracies.

How To Play ...

1) Have two or more people around (the more the better).

2) The person holding the book asks the question and the person listening HAS to answer one of the two options (no skipping).

3) Take turns asking questions (Don't keep the book to yourself).

4) That's it, have fun!

Would You Rather...

Step on dog's poop every time you go out OR have a bird poop on you every time you go out?

⸺⸺⸺⸺⸺⸺⸺⟶

Have to brush your teeth with shampoo OR wash your hair with toothpaste?

Would You Rather...

Have some wet dog food with your dinner OR eat your cereal with condensed coconut cream instead of milk?

―――――――――▶

Fart a little every time you laugh OR spit on the person next to you every time you cough?

Would You Rather...

Use your butt to eat OR use your mouth to poop?

⟶

Bathe in dead cockroaches OR shower in saliva?

Would You Rather...

Buy all your underwear second hand OR buy all your toothbrushes used?

Have a gremlin living in your locker at school that pees on all your books OR a gremlin that lives under your bed and cries every night?

Would You Rather...

Announce that you have to pee every time you need to go to the bathroom OR announce whenever you feel like you need to fart?

Fall from the roof into a dumpster of old diapers but not get injured OR fall into a bouncy castle and break your arm?

Would You Rather...

Eat a bowl of cat food if it made you super smart OR eat a bowl of soggy bread in milk if it made you super funny?

Have long, yellow fingernails like a witch OR short, cracked fingernails like a goblin?

Would You Rather...

Be caught wiping your boogers on someone else's sofa OR be heard farting in the library when it's dead silent?

Slip and fall into a puddle of sewer water OR step in a pile of crunchy snake skins?

Would You Rather...

Have massive ears that allow you to fly like Dumbo OR have long giraffe legs that allow you to run incredibly fast?

Have a unicorn horn on the top of your head OR have a hairy monkey chest?

Would You Rather...

Have one hand the size of a baseball glove OR one foot the size of a cupcake?

Have the same haircut forever OR wear the same clothes forever?

Would You Rather...

Find out you have rats living under your house OR there's a nest of tarantulas hidden in your room?

———————————▶

Have your ears replaced with donkey ears OR have your eyes replaced with camel eyes?

Would You Rather...

Lick your neighbor's toes OR let a stranger lick your toes?

Have your face turn blue when you are stressed OR have your body sweat and your shirt gets wet all over when you are worried?

Would You Rather...

Kiss a dog on the lips OR lick the back of a frog?

———————————▶

Wear your teacher's clothes for a whole week OR have your teacher's voice for the week?

Would You Rather...

Eat a piece of fruit from the garbage OR drink an expired carton of custard?

Have a long tongue that can touch your ear OR another nose on the back of your head for extra smell?

Would You Rather...

Immediately forget someone's name when you meet a new person OR sneeze on them when they say their name?

———————————————▶

Eat two rotten avocados on toast OR eat a muesli bar made from insect protein?

Would You Rather...

Kiss a pig on the cheek OR put a string of a dirty mop in your mouth for three seconds?

Have the nails on your hands never stop growing without being able to cut them OR the nails on your feet never stop growing without being able to cut them?

Would You Rather...

Eat a curry made from rat OR spend a day in prison?

Burn everything you cook OR put too much salt in everything you cook?

Would You Rather...

Have two belly buttons OR four nipples?

Be covered in fish scales and be able to swim extra fast OR have cheetah spots and be able to run extra fast?

Would You Rather...

Have pink colored blood and have to donate blood once a week OR black teeth and never have to go to the dentist?

⸻

Get a lifetime supply of your favorite food by sitting in a box with mini scorpions for a minute OR get your kitchen filled with that food by running half a marathon with no training?

Would You Rather...

Wash everyone else's clothes but never have to iron your own clothes OR iron everyone else's clothes but never have to wash your own?

Always get bitten by mosquitos but never get the flu OR get the flu once a month and never get any bug bites?

Would You Rather...

Have your whole body covered in freckles OR only have your hands covered with thick hair like an ape?

⬅————————➡

Add one scoop of cat food to everything you eat OR a hand full of cat hair to everything you eat?

Would You Rather...

Shave your head every year OR never wash your hair again?

⸻

Eat only round foods for a year OR foods that are extremely salty for a year?

Would You Rather...

Have fangs like a wolf OR a tongue like a snake?

Have a pig's tail and smell clean OR a lion's mane but smell like raw meat?

Would You Rather...

Escape a castle through an underwater passageway filled with sleeping crocodiles OR a rope bridge filled with evil apes?

Create the antidote for a terrible virus by infecting yourself but not have time to save yourself OR not create the antidote at all?

Would You Rather...

Have eagle wings that allow you to fly but you can't fit through any doorways OR gecko fingers that allow you to climb walls but you can't hold cups again and have to drink with your tongue?

Have medicine that makes you smell like onions OR medicine that tastes like raw onions?

Would You Rather...

Meet your favorite celebrity but you pee your pants when you meet them OR meet the President of the United States after you haven't had a shower for a week?

A wrinkled face like an eighty year old and a normal body OR a wrinkled, saggy body and a normal face?

Would You Rather...

Have the voice of a baby for the next month OR the voice of an old man who smokes twenty cigarettes a day for a month?

Work in a day care and have to change dirty diapers all day OR wear a diaper all day and not be able to change it?

Would You Rather...

Cook and eat all your meals for the next week outside over an open fire like a cave man OR be able to eat inside your home but raw meat only?

Drink all your drinks out of a shoe OR eat all your meals without any cutlery including rice, pasta and cereal?

Would You Rather...

Be in the same pool when ten others are peeing in it OR be in the pool when one other person throws up in it?

Lather yourself in cooking oil before sleeping every night OR rinse your mouth with coconut oil for twenty minutes before leaving the house every morning?

Would You Rather...

Get a kiss from someone with no teeth OR with someone with no lips?

Eat the paper napkin you use at a restaurant after finishing your meal OR have to lick clean the fingers of everyone at your table?

Would You Rather...

Drink a sip of water from a green colored pond OR a cup of milk that has been left out in the sun for four hours?

───────────▶

Have to throw your trash bags into the garbage truck every morning OR wash out the inside of the garbage truck once a month?

Would You Rather...

Only take a bath once a month OR take a bath everyday in someone else's used and dirty bath water?

Have brown colored sweat that smells like chocolate OR pink colored ear wax that tastes like cotton candy?

Would You Rather...

Have to unclog a sink that someone threw up in after eating hot dogs and onion rings OR clean a toilet after someone's had diarrhoea with spicy Chinese food?

⬅————————➡

Brush someone's hair that has lice and dandruff OR someone's hair who has dreadlocks and hasn't been washed in a year?

Would You Rather...

Have a constantly runny nose with green mucus OR not ever be able to clean the morning crust from your eyes?

Sleep on a mattress that is full of spider nests OR eat from a loaf of bread that has maggots?

Would You Rather...

Share your only pair of shoes with someone OR share your toothbrush?

⎯⎯⎯⎯⎯⎯⎯⎯⟶

Have the daily household chore of cleaning hair out of the shower drain with your bare hands OR cleaning food out of the kitchen sink drain with your bare hands?

Would You Rather...

Sit on the bus next to someone who kept sneezing on you OR in front of a baby who keeps pulling your hair?

Clean a dog's butt because it's got some poop left over OR brush a camel's tooth who's known for spitting a lot?

Would You Rather...

Be sprayed in the face by a rhino peeing OR hit in the face by a monkey throwing his poop?

⟵——————⟶

Eat a burger after it fell on a dirty floor OR eat a stack of pancakes with someone's finger nail in it?

Would You Rather...

Scrape your own knees OR change a dirty Band-Aid for someone else?

Have a problem where your skin constantly peels off OR a problem where your hair is constantly falling out?

Would You Rather...

Make lots of money for cleaning people's ears and nostrils OR make only a little bit of money for washing dogs?

―――――――――▶

Have visiting relatives who drink orange juice straight from the carton OR who loudly sip every drink they drink?

Would You Rather...

Your clothes be covered in itchy cat fur OR smelly dog fur?

⸻

Have bracelets around your wrists made from human teeth OR a necklace made from monkey fingers?

Would You Rather...

Be chased down the street by one hundred non-poisonous snakes OR by one rabid dog?

⟶

Always wear bright blue lipstick OR always have dry chapped lips?

Would You Rather...

Shrink into a dwarf every time you get wet OR grow into a giant every time you get angry?

Sit in the front row of a class where the teacher spits when they talk OR the back row under the air conditioner dripping slimy goo?

Would You Rather...

Put your hand into a fountain full of piranhas OR sleep in your room full of mosquitoes?

⎯⎯⎯⎯⎯⎯⎯⎯⎯⎯➤

Have to add gravy to all your food OR cinnamon to all your drinks?

Would You Rather...

Sit next to someone at the dinner table who keeps stealing food from your plate OR across from someone who talks with their mouth full?

Find a tooth in your mashed potatoes OR a spider in your sweet potatoes?

Would You Rather...

Brush your teeth with chocolate flavored toothpaste that looks like poo OR rinse your mouth with apple juice flavored mouth wash that looks like cat pee?

Always have glittery make up on your face like you've just come from a party OR big red boils on both your cheeks?

Would You Rather...

Extra long fingernails and toenails OR extra long earlobes and eyelashes?

───────────────▶

Have holes in all your socks and underwear OR in all your shirts and shorts?

Would You Rather...

All spiders are able to fly like birds but aren't poisonous OR all birds suddenly lose their wings and become vicious?

⎯⎯⎯⎯⎯⎯⎯⎯⟶

Get tangled in a giant spider's web OR fall into quick sand?

Would You Rather...

Get prank called everyday OR have someone leave a bag of dog poop on your porch once a week?

Go down a water slide into a pool of melted cheese that you can eat OR jump on a jumpy castle made out of marshmallows?

Would You Rather...

Have your hands superglued together like when you pray OR your knees glued together so you walk funny?

Be blindfolded with a baseball bat in a tiger enclosure OR handcuffed with no weapon in the same situation?

Would You Rather...

Fall on a prickly cactus in the desert OR have to eat a rattle snake to survive when stranded in a desert?

Climb Mount Everest knowing that you would get frostbite and lose three of your toes OR ride the biggest wave in a surf competition knowing you would stack it halfway through?

Would You Rather...

Be roommates with a cranky Irish leprechaun that won't stop talking smack OR with a sad birthday Clown that keeps crying when he laughs?

Fall into a pool of glue and then be sprayed with feathers OR have a hundred eggs thrown at you followed by ten kilos of flour?

Would You Rather...

Need to pee five minutes after every time you eat OR hiccup uncontrollably evertime you try to eat?

Have Dorito dust on your fingers for a whole year OR have to walk around in soggy wet socks for a year?

Would You Rather...

Sit on an extremely cold toilet seat OR on one that is slightly warm (someone else has just sat on it?)

⟵————————⟶

Have a dog with human hands and feet OR a cat with a human face?

Would You Rather...

Give up your favourite food forever OR wake up every morning with a 3% chance that you'll be completely covered in Nutella?

Have legs the size of your fingers OR fingers the size of your legs?

Would You Rather...

Eat a fresh tin of small cat food OR four brown rotten bananas?

Sleep for 3 months straight and not have to sleep for the rest of the year OR spend the week in a toilet and not have to go for the rest of the year?

Would You Rather...

Have 3 eyes and be able to see like an eagle OR 3 ears and hear like a bat?

Have three arms so you can get more work done quickly OR three legs that will make you run quicker?

Would You Rather...

No tongue so you can't taste OR no nose so you can't smell?

⟵――――――――――⟶

Have a constant red itch from a mosquito on your back that won't go away for the next month OR have constant pain in your stomach preventing you eating for a week?

Would You Rather...

Get stuck next to someone on the plane who can't stop burping OR can't stop farting?

Have the ability to transform your legs into wheels OR your hands into knives?

Would You Rather...

Be bitten by a thousand mosquitoes OR a hundred bees?

———————▶

Mow a soccer field with a pair of scissors OR scrub your whole toilet clean with a toothbrush?

Would You Rather...

Have hot pink hair for a month OR blue skin like a Smurf for a week?

Have a bunch of non venomous snakes slither around you in a box for five minutes OR a hundred cockroaches thrown on top of you?

Would You Rather...

Not be able to change your clothes for a week OR not be able to shower for a week?

⟵————————⟶

Be unattractive but always smell amazing OR look good and always smell bad?

Would You Rather...

Have a human brain but the body of a hamster OR a hamster brain and the body of a human?

———————————→

Have an extra eye on a finger so you can see things in hard to see areas OR extra taste buds on a finger to taste things before it goes in your mouth?

Would You Rather...

Accidentally puke on your favorite movie star OR be puked on by your favorite movie star?

———————————▶

Have to drink everything through your nose OR eat everything through your ears?

Would You Rather...

Always have your breath smelling like garlic OR sweat sticky honey all over your body when you get hot?

Have an extra pair of eyes on the back of your head OR one more eye on your belly button?

Would You Rather...

Only have three fingers on each of your hands OR ten toes on each foot?

———————————————▶

Swim in a cold pool made with ice cream OR have a bath in hot chocolate?

Would You Rather...

Eat a lollipop that taste like chili OR eat pancakes that tastes like cabbage?

Have to lick the sole of your shoes OR lick the inside bit of a trash cans lid?

Would You Rather...

Have to smell a skunk every time you wake up OR eat a worm every time you go to bed?

⎯⎯⎯⎯⎯⎯⎯⎯⎯⎯⎯⟶

Hold a prickly porcupine for a minute OR pick up a live crab and move it from one box to another?

Would You Rather...

Drink clear water that tastes like soap OR soap looking water that tastes normal?

Always eat a piece of fruit that has had a worm in it OR never be able to eat a fruit again?

Would You Rather...

Have to smell all your classmates socks after doing sports OR wear one of the pairs for a day?

⟵——————————⟶

Have carrot flavored ice cream with a strawberry flavored cone OR cheese flavored ice cream with a pistachio flavored cone?

Would You Rather...

Remove someone else's earwax OR remove lice from someone else's hair?

⟶

Have sweaty armpits but not be able to wash them for a month OR dirty hands but not be able to wash them for a week?

Would You Rather...

Drink a protein shake made of eggs and snails OR eat some cooked snake skin in a curry?

Smell like rotten fish every time you do sports OR smell like burnt bread every time you get sick?

Would You Rather...

Have earwax coming out of your nose OR have boogers coming out of your ears?

⎯⎯⎯⎯⎯⎯⎯⎯⎯⎯→

Get stuck in the boogers of a giant OR in the stomach of a whale?

Would You Rather...

Have a nose twice its normal size OR have a tail like a horse?

Eat the food you hate the most every day for a year OR eat pizza and find someone else's hair in it?

Would You Rather...

Have to use your socks as toilet paper OR mayonnaise as shampoo?

———————————→

Have rotten eggs for breakfast every day for a week OR have mouldy bread everyday for a week?

Would You Rather...

Have Christmas cookies dipped in onion sauce OR drink a cup of hot cocoa with crickets inside?

⬅——————————➡

Decorate your Christmas tree with glimmering boogers of a giant OR with dead insects?

Would You Rather...

Eat a soy sauce flavoured popsicle OR a mustard flavoured biscuit?

Have a salad made with grasshoppers OR a smoothie made with worms?

Would You Rather...

Get a hug from someone who is sweaty OR someone who is stinky?

Drink a gallon of pickle juice and then get to eat all the McDonald's you want OR drink half a gallon prune juice and get nothing after?

Would You Rather...

Live as a tiny person among a world of giants OR live as a giant in a world of tiny people?

Have the right half of your body smaller than the left half OR the lower half of your body smaller than the top half?

The End

www.ingramcontent.com/pod-product-compliance
Lightning Source LLC
Chambersburg PA
CBHW071028080526
44587CB00015B/2534